NATIONAL GEOGRAPHIC KiDS

weird but true! 8

THAT'S WEIRD!

THE CROWNED SIFAKA— A **LEMUR** THAT LIVES IN MADAGASCAR— EATS **DIRT**.

NATIONAL
GEOGRAPHIC
KiDS

# weird but true! 8

## 300 outrageous facts

NATIONAL GEOGRAPHIC
WASHINGTON, D.C.

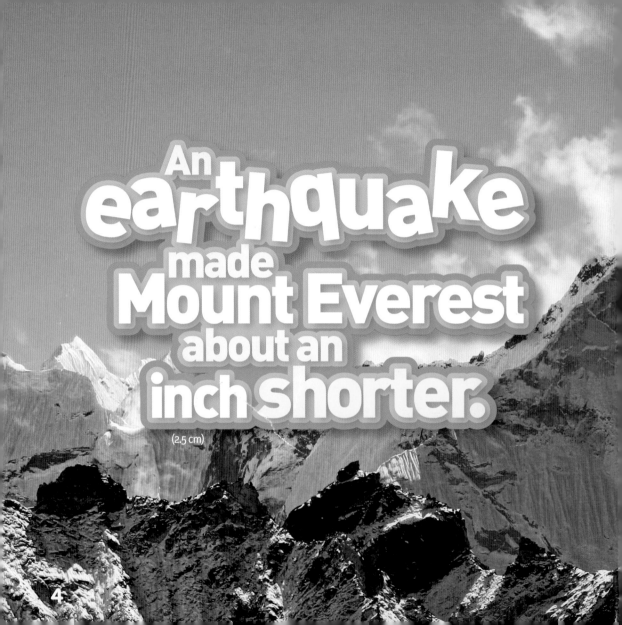

An **earthquake** made **Mount Everest** about an **inch shorter.**

(2.5 cm)

4

NATIONAL GEOGRAPHIC KiDS

weird but true! 8

300 outrageous facts

NATIONAL GEOGRAPHIC
WASHINGTON, D.C.

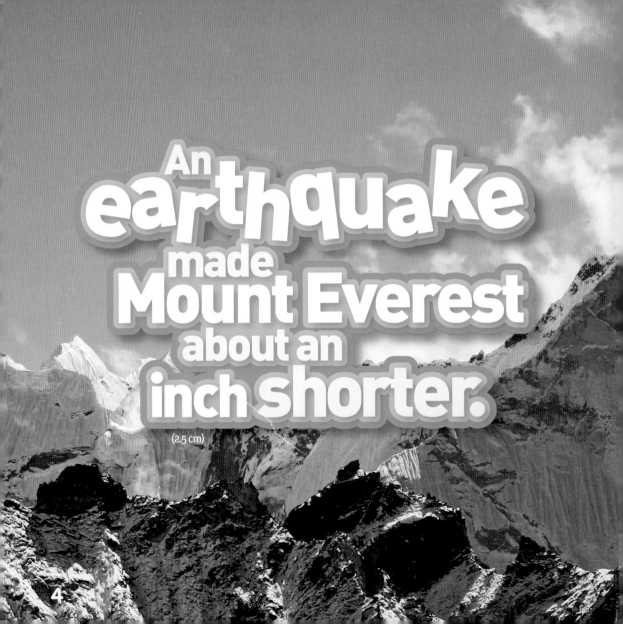

An **earthquake** made **Mount Everest** about an **inch shorter.**

(2.5 cm)

5

There are as many molecules in **ten drops** of **water** as there are **stars** in the **universe.**

KANGAROOS USE THEIR TAILS AS AN EXTRA LEG WHEN WALKING.

SCIENTISTS BUILT A FISH-SHAPED MICRO-ROBOT THAT IS SMALLER THAN A HUMAN HAIR.

ONLY ABOUT **10 PERCENT** OF THE POPULATION IS LEFT-HANDED.

Drinking **coffee** in 17th-century Turkey was punishable by **death.**

YOUR BODY'S SMELL—OR "**ODORPRINT**"—IS AS UNIQUE AS YOUR FINGERPRINTS.

A **FARMER** FROM MASSACHUSETTS, U.S.A., ONCE PADDLED DOWN A RIVER IN AN **817-POUND** (371-kg) HOLLOWED-OUT PUMPKIN.

MORE PEOPLE ARE KILLED EACH YEAR **BY DOMESTIC PIGS THAN BY SHARKS.**

DANGER IS MY MIDDLE NAME.

YOU NEED A **FOOT-LONG STICK,** (0.3-m) A **THREE-POUND PUCK,** (1.4-kg) AND **SNORKEL GEAR** TO **PLAY** UNDERWATER HOCKEY.

A compound in **human spit** can help **heal wounds.**

Scientists use a **barfing machine** and fake vomit to help them study how **viruses** spread through the air.

The planet Mercury is shrinking.

LUKE SKYWALKER'S **LIGHTSABER** HAS ACTUALLY BEEN TO **SPACE.**

ONE MAN OWNS 500,000 PIECES OF *STAR WARS*

The sound of **Darth Vader's breathing** was inspired by breathing apparatuses used for **scuba diving.**

A WATERFALL IN MINNESOTA, U.S.A., DROPS INTO A DEEP HOLE AND DISAPPEARS. NO ONE KNOWS WHERE THE WATER GOES.

# A GIANT BLACK HOLE ATE A STAR AND BURPED OUT A FLAME.

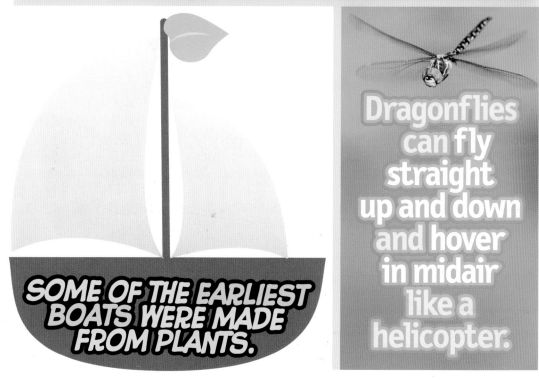

SOME OF THE EARLIEST BOATS WERE MADE FROM PLANTS.

Dragonflies can fly straight up and down and hover in midair like a helicopter.

A NOW EXTINCT FROG SPECIES SWALLOWED ITS EGGS, INCUBATED THEM IN ITS STOMACH, AND GAVE BIRTH THROUGH ITS MOUTH.

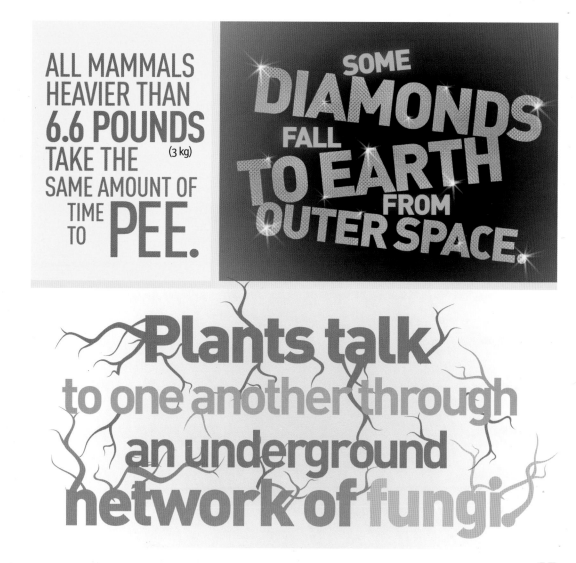

ALL MAMMALS HEAVIER THAN **6.6 POUNDS** (3 kg) TAKE THE SAME AMOUNT OF TIME TO **PEE.**

SOME **DIAMONDS FALL TO EARTH FROM OUTER SPACE.**

**Plants talk** to one another through an underground **network of fungi.**

A **FARMER** FROM MASSACHUSETTS, U.S.A., ONCE PADDLED DOWN A RIVER IN AN **817-POUND** (371-kg) HOLLOWED-OUT **PUMPKIN.**

# MORE PEOPLE ARE KILLED EACH YEAR BY DOMESTIC PIGS THAN BY SHARKS.

YOU NEED A **FOOT-LONG STICK,** (0.3-m) A **THREE-POUND PUCK,** (1.4-kg) AND **SNORKEL GEAR** TO **PLAY** UNDERWATER HOCKEY.

ONLY ABOUT **10 PERCENT** OF THE POPULATION IS LEFT-HANDED.

Drinking *coffee* in 17th-century *Turkey* was punishable by *death*.

YOUR BODY'S SMELL—OR "ODORPRINT"—IS AS UNIQUE AS YOUR FINGERPRINTS.

WEEEE!

As part of a **beaver-relocation effort,** 76 beavers once **parachuted** into the Idaho, U.S.A., wilderness.

19

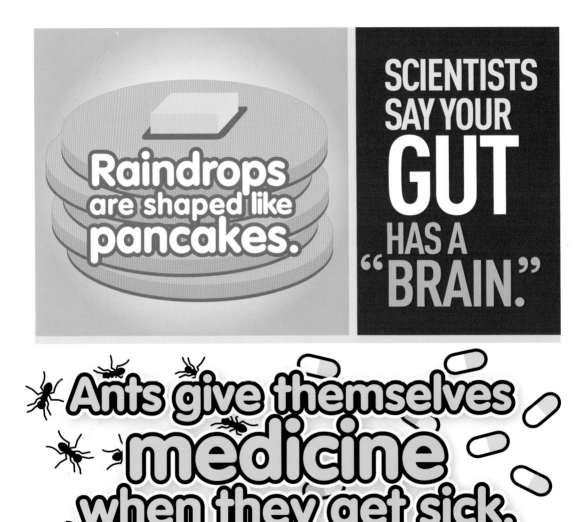

Raindrops are shaped like pancakes.

SCIENTISTS SAY YOUR GUT HAS A "BRAIN."

Ants give themselves medicine when they get sick.

Lightning almost never strikes the North or South Poles.

LIGHTNING STRIKES MEN MORE OFTEN THAN IT DOES WOMEN.

NEWBORN TASMANIAN DEVILS ARE THE SIZE OF A RAISIN.

Jellyfish invasions have shut down nuclear power plants.

There's an app that lets people **rent** out their **toilets.**

SCIENTISTS FOUND **PREHISTORIC VIRUSES** IN **SIBERIAN ICE.**

A 16th-century *astronomer* lost part of his **nose** in a duel about *math.*

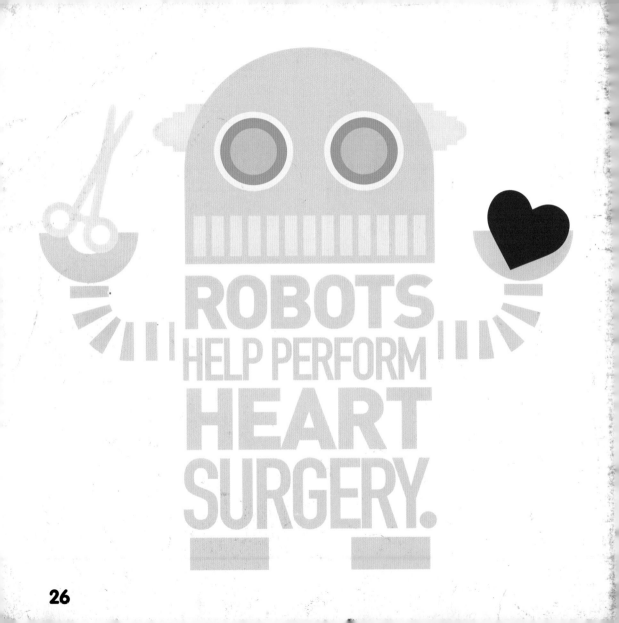

ROBOTS HELP PERFORM HEART SURGERY.

THE HUBBLE SPACE TELESCOPE CAN LOOK BACK IN TIME.

Mushrooms are also called toadstools.

# NEANDERTHALS FLOSSED THEIR TEETH WITH TWIGS AND BLADES OF GRASS.

peecycling = using urine to fertilize vegetables

## RESEARCHERS HAVE DEVELOPED 3-D GLASSES FOR INSECTS.

A STUDY FOUND THAT **CHILDREN** WHOSE FAMILIES **WASH DISHES BY HAND** HAVE **FEWER ALLERGIES** THAN KIDS WHOSE FAMILIES **USE A DISHWASHER.**

**Wolf pups can't see or hear when they're born.**

A STUDY FOUND THAT **CHILDREN** WHOSE FAMILIES WASH DISHES BY HAND HAVE FEWER ALLERGIES THAN KIDS WHOSE FAMILIES USE A DISHWASHER.

**Wolf pups can't see or hear when they're born.**

You are made of star dust.

Some plants can hear themselves being eaten.

There was only one student in New Mexico State University's first graduating class.

SCIENTISTS THINK **T. REX** WAS A CANNIBAL.

There are approximately **3 trillion** (3,000,000,000,000) trees on Earth.

# ONE RARE PLANT GROWS ONLY ON TOP OF DIAMOND DEPOSITS.

**THAT'S WEIRD**

A **BROWN BAT** CAN EAT **1,000 MOSQUITOES** IN AN HOUR.

*People in one small Turkish town communicate over long distances by* **whistling.**

A MAN SUED THE KELLOGG COMPANY BECAUSE HE FOUND NO REAL FRUIT IN HIS FROOT LOOPS CEREAL.

Some **carnivorous plants** can **eat** birds.

During his 1905 U.S. presidential inauguration, *Teddy Roosevelt* wore *a ring* containing a lock of **Abraham Lincoln's** *hair.*

Your brain produces enough **electricity** to power a 40-watt **lightbulb** for an entire **day.**

HUMMINGBIRDS USE **HAWKS** FOR PROTECTION.

moonbow=

a nighttime rainbow

41

Early **rugby balls** were made from **inflated pigs' bladders.**

2015 was the International Year of Light.

SCIENTISTS HAVE DISCOVERED A **PROTEIN** THAT CAN PREVENT **ICE CREAM** FROM **MELTING** QUICKLY IN HOT WEATHER.

# THE BOARD GAME MONOPOLY

WAS ORIGINALLY CALLED
THE LANDLORD'S GAME.

**MONOPOLY**
IS BASED ON
**STREET NAMES**
IN ATLANTIC CITY,
NEW JERSEY, U.S.A.

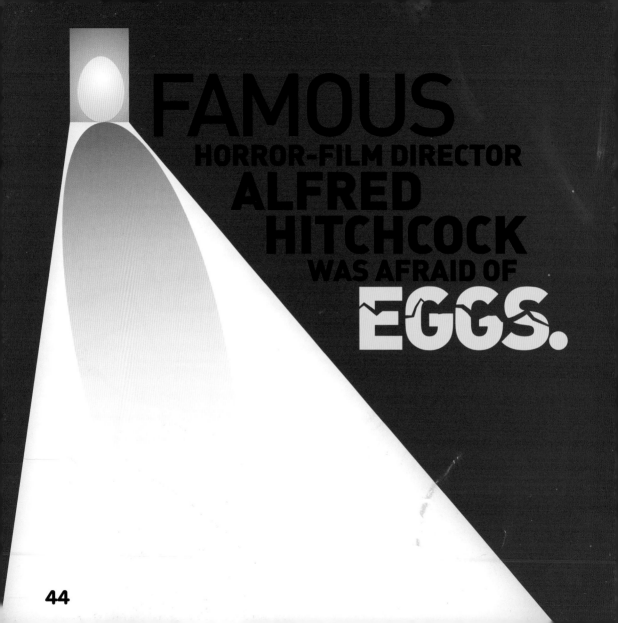

**FAMOUS**
HORROR-FILM DIRECTOR
**ALFRED**
**HITCHCOCK**
WAS AFRAID OF
**EGGS.**

44

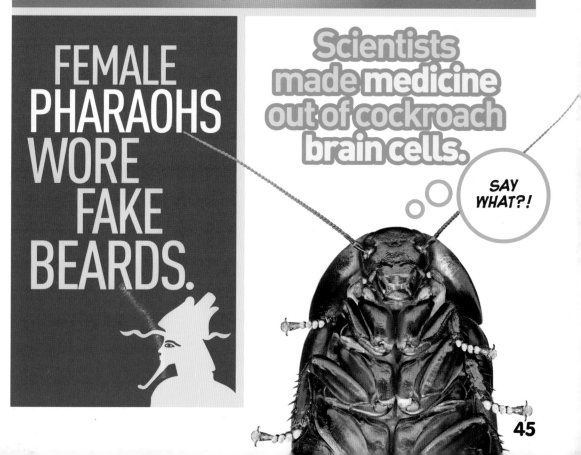

U.S. president *James A. Garfield* was fond of **squirrel soup.**

FEMALE **PHARAOHS** WORE FAKE BEARDS.

Scientists made medicine out of cockroach brain cells.

SAY WHAT?!

45

# Elephants have fingers on the end of their trunks.

POPE LEO X **BURIED** HIS

AN ELEPHANT'S
TOOTH
IS THE SIZE
OF A BRICK.

PET ELEPHANT **UNDER** THE VATICAN.

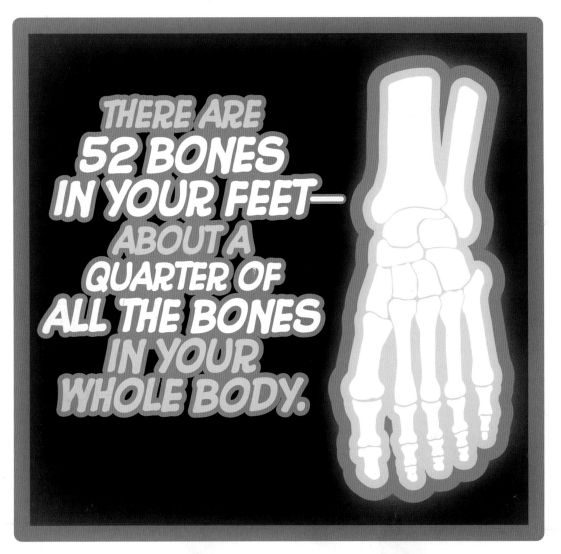

THERE ARE 52 BONES IN YOUR FEET— ABOUT A QUARTER OF ALL THE BONES IN YOUR WHOLE BODY.

VANILLA IS USED TO MAKE CHOCOLATE.

Some dogs' paws smell like corn chips.

AFTER THEIR 1972 NATIONAL HOCKEY LEAGUE WIN, THE BOSTON BRUINS'S NAME WAS MISSPELLED "BQSTQN BRUINS" ON THE STANLEY CUP.

THERE'S A ROCK ON MARS THAT LOOKS LIKE A FLOATING SPOON.

AN EAR OF CORN CAN HAVE UP TO 1,200 KERNELS.

A LIBROCUBICULARIST IS SOMEONE WHO READS IN BED.

Police "arrested" a goat for loitering outside a doughnut shop in Saskatchewan, Canada.

There are more than 40,000 types of rice.

If you strung together all the **cranberries** grown in North America **in one year,** they would stretch from Boston to Los Angeles, U.S.A., more than **500 times.**

SHEEP SHEARING IS A COMPETITIVE SPORT.

THERE IS A
BODY OF
WATER

FLOATING IN
OUTER SPACE
THAT'S
140 TRILLION
TIMES
BIGGER

THAN ALL THE
EARTH'S
OCEANS
COMBINED.

A GERMAN ROBOT LEARNED
HOW TO MAKE PANCAKES.

PR2

**penny farthing**= a bicycle with a giant **front wheel** and a **tiny back wheel**

During Olympic training, **swimmer Michael Phelps** consumed more than **12,000 calories** a day—about the equivalent of **80 cups of whole milk.** (18.9 L)

**TOMATOES CAN BE PURPLE.**

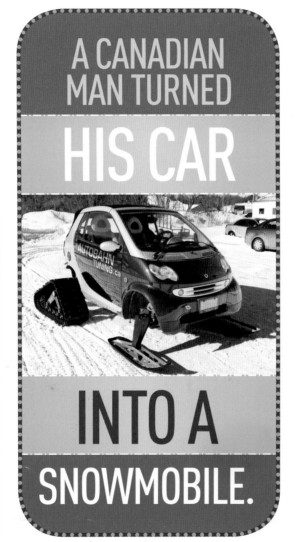

A CANADIAN MAN TURNED

HIS CAR

INTO A

SNOWMOBILE.

**Fastest one-mile run** (1.6-km) **by a human wearing swim fins 5 minutes and 48.86 seconds**

**CHRISTOPHER COLUMBUS** BROUGHT THE FIRST **LEMON SEEDS** TO THE AMERICAS.

PARTS OF CALIFORNIA, U.S.A., ARE SINKING.

IN NEW ZEALAND, PARENTS AREN'T ALLOWED TO NAME THEIR BABIES AFTER PUNCTUATION MARKS.

" ! ? ; - , ( : ) [ , ] ' { . . . }.

# A HONEYBEE HAS THE SAME NUMBER OF HAIRS AS A SQUIRREL: THREE MILLION.

HONEY
HAS BEEN FOUND
IN THE
CENTER OF OLD
GOLF BALLS.

THAT COULD ARTIFICIALLY POLLINATE CROPS.

There's a **comet** shaped like a **rubber duck.**

CHOCOLATE WAS ONCE USED AS MONEY.

Some **snakes pass gas** in **self-defense.**

# Painting

## was once an

## Olympic event.

**One in four medicines comes from rain forest plants.**

The world's first speeding **ticket** was given to a motorist going **eight miles** an hour.
(12.9 km/h)

The 1904 World's Fair featured a life-size elephant made of almonds.

**BACTERIA TALK TO EACH OTHER.**

"chicken wing" = a bad golf swing

The city of Redondo Beach, California, U.S.A., once chose a **blimp** as its official bird.

**SNAILS SMELL WITH THEIR LIPS.**

69

TO ENSURE THEY HAVEN'T BEEN SWITCHED OR TAMPERED WITH, ALL EGGS USED IN THE COMPETITIVE SPORT OF EGG THROWING ARE MARKED FOR SECURITY PURPOSES.

"FRIED EGG"=THE WAY A GOLF

SCIENTISTS HAVE FIGURED OUT HOW TO UNBOIL AN EGG.

BALL SOMETIMES LANDS IN A SAND TRAP

Humans and dogs perform together in a sport called musical canine freestyle.

Einstein never wore socks.

Earmuffs were invented by a teenage boy in 1858.

# Some orchids smell like human body odor to attract mosquitoes.

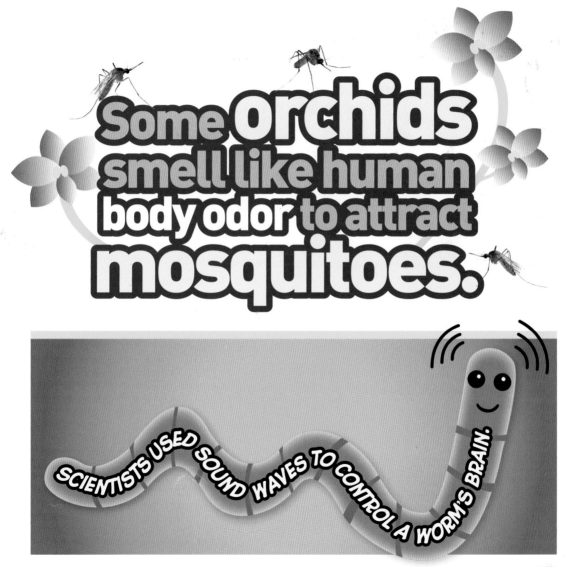

SCIENTISTS USED SOUND WAVES TO CONTROL A WORM'S BRAIN.

DEATH METAL MUSIC ATTRACTS SHARKS.

IN NEW ZEALAND, YOU CAN **PLAY GOLF** WITH **FOOTBALL-SHAPED** GOLF BALLS.

Some scientists think that **plants** can learn.

Spiders can build **webs** that are a half mile long.

(0.8 km)

An artist created an **18-foot-long** (5.5-m) **Batmobile** out of more than **500,000** Lego bricks.

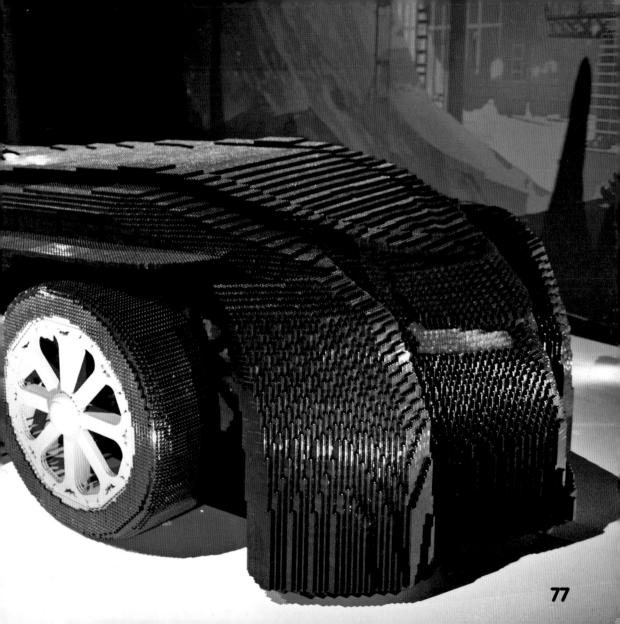

Tooth enamel evolved from ancient fish scales.

An **aglet** is the plastic piece at the end of your shoelace.

Fidgeting can make you healthier.

**snood** = the flesh that hangs down over a male turkey's beak

# THE LONGEST PIZZA

EVER MADE WAS ALMOST A MILE LONG.
(1.6 km)

IT WAS MADE WITH 1.5 TONS (1.4 t) OF MOZZARELLA AND 2 TONS (1.8 t) OF TOMATO SAUCE.

GLOBAL WARMING IS CHANGING THE SHAPE OF THE PLANET.

80